Dalgleish

AF086341

by Iain Gray

PUBLISHING

WRITING *to* REMEMBER

79 Main Street, Newtongrange,
Midlothian EH22 4NA
Tel: 0131 344 0414   Fax: 0845 075 6085
E-mail: info@lang-syne.co.uk
www.langsyneshop.co.uk

Design by Dorothy Meikle
Printed by Printwell Ltd
© Lang Syne Publishers Ltd 2021

All rights reserved. No part of this publication may be reproduced, stored or introduced into a retrieval system, or transmitted in any form or by any means (electronic, mechanical, photocopying, recording or otherwise) without the prior written permission of Lang Syne Publishers Ltd.

ISBN 978-1-85217-770-6

Dalgleish

MOTTO:
My delight

CREST:
An open book

TERRITORY:
The Borders

NAME VARIATIONS include:
Daglish
Dalglese
Dalglish
Dagleishe
Dalgleise
Dalgis
Dalgiss

Chapter one:

The origins of the clan system

by Rennie McOwan

The original Scottish clans of the Highlands and the great families of the Lowlands and Borders were gatherings of families, relatives, allies and neighbours for mutual protection against rivals or invaders.

Scotland experienced invasion from the Vikings, the Romans and English armies from the south. The Norman invasion of what is now England also had an influence on land-holding in Scotland. Some of these invaders stayed on and in time became 'Scottish'.

The word clan derives from the Gaelic language term 'clann', meaning children, and it was first used many centuries ago as communities were formed around tribal lands in glens and mountain fastnesses.

The format of clans changed over the centuries, but at its best the chief and his family held the land on behalf of all, like trustees, and the ordinary clansmen and women believed they had a blood relationship with the founder of their clan.

There were two way duties and obligations. An inadequate chief could be deposed and replaced by someone of greater ability.

Clan people had an immense pride in race. Their relationship with the chief was like adult children to a father and they had a real dignity.

The concept of clanship is very old and a more feudal notion of authority gradually crept in.

Pictland, for instance, was divided into seven principalities ruled by feudal leaders who were the strongest and most charismatic leaders of their particular groups.

By the sixth century the 'British' kingdoms of Strathclyde, Lothian and Celtic Dalriada (Argyll) had emerged and Scotland, as one nation, began to take shape in the time of King Kenneth MacAlpin.

Some chiefs claimed descent from ancient kings which may not have been accurate in every case.

By the twelfth and thirteenth centuries the clans and families were more strongly brought under the central control of Scottish monarchs.

Lands were awarded and administered more and more under royal favour, yet the power of the area clan chiefs was still very great.

The long wars to ensure Scotland's

independence against the expansionist ideas of English monarchs extended the influence of some clans and reduced the lands of others.

Those who supported Scotland's greatest king, Robert the Bruce, were awarded the territories of the families who had opposed his claim to the Scottish throne.

In the Scottish Borders country – the notorious Debatable Lands – the great families built up a ferocious reputation for providing warlike men accustomed to raiding into England and occasionally fighting one another.

Chiefs had the power to dispense justice and to confiscate lands and clan warfare produced a society where martial virtues – courage, hardiness, tenacity – were greatly admired.

Gradually the relationship between the clans and the Crown became strained as Scottish monarchs became more orientated to life in the Lowlands and, on occasion, towards England.

The Highland clans spoke a different language, Gaelic, whereas the language of Lowland Scotland and the court was Scots and in more modern times, English.

Highlanders dressed differently, had different

customs, and their wild mountain land sometimes seemed almost foreign to people living in the Lowlands.

It must be emphasised that Gaelic culture was very rich and story-telling, poetry, piping, the clarsach (harþ) and other music all flourished and were greatly respected.

Highland culture was different from other parts of Scotland but it was not inferior or less sophisticated.

Central Government, whether in London or Edinburgh, sometimes saw the Gaelic clans as a challenge to their authority and some sent expeditions into the Highlands and west to crush the power of the Lords of the Isles.

Nevertheless, when the eighteenth century Jacobite Risings came along the cause of the Stuarts was mainly supported by Highland clans.

The word Jacobite comes from the Latin for James – Jacobus. The Jacobites wanted to restore the exiled Stuarts to the throne of Britain.

The monarchies of Scotland and England became one in 1603 when King James VI of Scotland (1st of England) gained the English throne after Queen Elizabeth died.

The Union of Parliaments of Scotland and England, the Treaty of Union, took place in 1707.

Some Highland clans, of course, and Lowland families opposed the Jacobites and supported the incoming Hanoverians.

After the Jacobite cause finally went down at Culloden in 1746 a kind of ethnic cleansing took place. The power of the chiefs was curtailed. Tartan and the pipes were banned in law.

Many emigrated, some because they wanted to, some because they were evicted by force. In addition, many Highlanders left for the cities of the south to seek work.

Many of the clan lands became home to sheep and deer shooting estates.

But the warlike traditions of the clans and the great Lowland and Border families lived on, with their descendants fighting bravely for freedom in two world wars.

Remember the men from whence you came, says the Gaelic proverb, and to that could be added the role of many heroic women.

The spirit of the clan, of having roots, whether Highland or Lowland, means much to thousands of people.

Meanwhile, many families proudly boast the heraldic device known as a Coat of Arms,.

The central motif of the Coat of Arms would originally have been what was sometimes borne on the shield of a warrior to distinguish himself from others on the battlefield.

Clan warfare produced a society where courage and tenacity were greatly admired

Chapter two:

Moss troopers

A locational surname, 'Dalgleish' is readily identified with the local authority area formerly known as Selkirkshire, in the Scottish Borders.

More specifically, this early territory of bearers of the name and its numerous spelling variants is in the parish of Ettrick, above the sources of the Tinna Water.

Derived from the Gaelic 'dail', denoting 'field' and 'glas' indicating 'green', it is recorded in the form of 'Dalginge' in 1177 when a Nessus de (of) Dalginge witnessed a transaction involving a gift to the nuns of Berwick.

In yet another spelling variant, Symon de Dalgle is recorded as witnessing a charter in 1407, his son Simon of Dalgles serving in the church as a canon at Askirk in 1448 and Sir William de Dalgles in the role in 1452 of steward to the bishop of Glasgow and, later, to King James II.

But while these early bearers of the name so closely associated with the Borders achieved distinction because of their loyalty to both Church and Crown, others were notorious for their lawlessness.

Among the feared body of families known as riding clans, or reivers, they took this name from their time-honoured custom of reiving, or raiding, not only their neighbours' livestock but also that of their counterparts across the border.

The word 'bereaved', for example, indicating to have suffered loss, derives from the original 'reived', meaning to have suffered loss of property.

A constant thorn in the flesh of both the English and Scottish authorities was the cross-border raiding and pillaging carried out by well-mounted and heavily armed men, the contingent from the Scottish side of the border known and feared as 'moss troopers.'

In an attempt to bring order to what was known as the wild 'debateable land' on both sides of the border, King Alexander II of Scotland had in 1237 signed the Treaty of York, which for the first time established the Scottish border with England as a line running from the Solway to the Tweed.

On either side of the border there were three 'marches' or areas of administration, the West, East, and Middle Marches, and a warden governed these.

Complaints from either side of the border

were dealt with on Truce Days, when the wardens of the different marches would act as arbitrators.

There was also a law known as the Hot Trod, that granted anyone who had their livestock stolen the right to pursue the thieves and recover their property.

The post of March Warden was a powerful and lucrative one, with rival families vying for the position, and the marches became virtually a law unto themselves.

In the Scottish borderlands, the Homes and Swintons dominated the East March, while the Armstrongs, Maxwells, Johnstones, and Grahams were the rulers of the West March and the Kerrs, along with the Douglases and Elliots, held sway in the Dalgleish territory of the Middle March.

Wardens from the East Marches met at Redden Burn, on the Tweed, just west of Wark, while wardens for the Middle Marches met at Deadwater, on the North Tyne.

In about 1507, John Dalgleis of that Ilk and others of the name were pardoned for previous transgressions – but appear to have remained recalcitrant.

It is highly probable, for example, that it is this 'John Dalgleis' who is recorded in 1510, under the name 'John Dalglese', as being hanged for involvement in the burning of the Border settlements of Ancrum and Branxholm.

In 1594 the Scottish parliament drew up a series of harsh measures to suppress the lawless Border clans and families.

But the state of affairs was no better by 1608, when a Privy Council report graphically described how the 'wild incests, adulteries, convocation of the lieges, shooting and wearing of hackbuts, pistols, lances, daily bloodshed, oppression, and disobedience in civil matters, neither are nor has been punished.'

Their final death knell came in the early seventeenth century during the reign of King James I (King James VI of Scotland), when many were dispersed in the 'plantation' of what is now Northern Ireland by Protestants deemed more loyal to the Crown than the 'rebellious' native Irish.

But many, including bearers of the Dalgleish name, remained.

That Ettrick, meanwhile, is their original territory can be found on the landscape today in the place names Nether Dalgleish and Upper Dalgleish.

The village of Ettrick lies about 17 miles (28km) southwest of the county town of Selkirk, one of Scotland's oldest royal burghs and where its good citizens are fondly known as 'Souters', referring to the trade of cobblers, or shoe makers and menders.

The town and its environs are steeped in history, with associations that include the antiquarian and great man of letters Sir Walter Scott and the poet, essayist and novelist James Hogg, born at a farm within Ettrick parish in 1770.

A friend and contemporary of Scott and better known as the Ettrick Shepherd and author of the classic *The Private Memoirs and Confessions of a Justified Sinner*, he died in 1835 and is buried in Ettrick Kirkyard.

In the present day, Selkirk is home to the internationally renowned tartan design and weaving company D.C. Dalgleish.

The world's last artisan weaving mill utilising traditional 'flying shuttle' looms and in existence for more than 70 years, its future was secured in 2011 when taken over by Scotweb, of Edinburgh.

Travelling back much further in time, the Selkirk area and its families such as the Dalgleishes were embroiled for centuries in some of Scotland's pivotal events, including the Wars of Scottish Independence from 1296 to 1328 and 1332 to 1357.

Chapter three:

Flowers of the forest

Situated as they were on the Borders, the Dalgleishes, in common with others of their kind, were literally on the frontline of the Wars of Independence that frequently laid waste to their lands.

In 1296, a number of Scots were among the signatories to a humiliating treaty of fealty, the *Ragman Roll*, to England's conquering King Edward I, feared and loathed as the 'Hammer of the Scots'.

Signed by 1,500 earls, bishops, and burgesses, the parchment is known as the *Ragman Roll* because of the profusion of ribbons that dangle from the seals of the signatories.

With Scotland under the iron grip of English occupation at the time, those who signed had little option but to do so – but the humiliation was avenged when William Wallace sparked off a revolt in May of 1297, after slaying Sir William Heselrig, Sheriff of Lanark.

An expert in the tactics of guerrilla warfare, Wallace led his hardened band of freedom fighters on a series of lightning campaigns that inflicted stunning defeats on the English garrisons.

One of Wallace's many temporary headquarters was located in the near-impenetrable depths of Ettrick Forest and also Selkirk Forest, and among his fellow 'bravehearts' were Dalgleishes who knew every hidden pathway.

The great freedom fighter's campaigns culminated in the liberation of practically all of Scotland following the battle of Stirling Bridge, on September 11, 1297.

It was shortly after this victory that he was appointed Guardian of the Realm of Scotland and accordingly knighted in a ceremony conducted near Selkirk at what was known as the Kirk of the Forest.

A geophysics study conducted by archaeologists in 2016 suggests the site of the kirk was on what are now the ruins of the Auld Kirk, Selkirk.

Dr Chris Bowles, archaeologist for Scottish Borders Council, said: "Ruins of the Auld Kirk date from the 18th century, but we know this had replaced earlier churches on the site from the 12th and 16th centuries.

"We had been expecting the geophysics survey to uncover a 16th century church that we know to have existed and which was a replacement to the medieval church, but the only evidence in the survey is to the medieval church.

"The association between Wallace and the local area is quite well documented, with Wallace using guerrilla tactics to fight the English from Ettrick Forest.

"The Scottish nobles made Wallace Guardian of Scotland in recognition of his military successes."

Wallace was defeated the battle of Falkirk in July of 1298 and he was eventually betrayed and captured in August of 1305 – and, on August 23 of that year, brutally executed in London on the orders of a vengeful Edward.

Edward had hoped that Wallace's gruesome fate would serve as an example to others and discourage further revolt against English occupation of Scotland, but it only served to further enrage and inflame patriotic passion.

Robert the Bruce, who was enthroned as King of Scots at Scone in March of 1306, took up the banner of revolt again, and among his stalwart supporters were the Dalgleishes –also in the ranks of the Scots army that memorably defeated King Edward II at the battle of Bannockburn in 1314.

In 1513, the Dalgleishes were among the

5,000 Scots including King James IV, an archbishop, two bishops, eleven earls, fifteen barons, and 300 knights killed at the battle of Flodden, on Branxton Moor, Northumberland.

The Scottish monarch had embarked on the venture after Queen Anne of France, under the terms of the Auld Alliance between Scotland and her nation, appealed to him to 'break a lance' on her behalf and act as her chosen knight.

Crossing the border into England at the head of a 25,000-strong army, James engaged a 20,000-strong force commanded by the Earl of Surrey.

Despite their numerical superiority and bravery, however, the Scots proved no match for the skilled English artillery and superior military tactics of Surrey.

The disaster that was Flodden is annually commemorated through the Selkirk Common Riding, celebrating the burgh's ancient heritage and traditions.

Featuring up to 400 riders, the Riding marks how the first news of the defeat came from a local man named Fletcher, badly wounded and bearing a captured English regimental flag.

Riding into the town, he cast the bloodied flag around his head and then fell dead from his horse.

The grief of men and women at the loss of their menfolk is recalled in the haunting ballad *The Flooers o' the Forest – The Flowers of the Forest –* lamenting how they were all 'weeded away' and whose final verse, in Scots, is:

> *The English for ance, by*
> *guile wan the day,*
> *The Flooers o' the Forest,*
> *that fought aye the*
> *foremost,*
> *The pride o' oor land lie*
> *cauld in the clay*

One infamous bearer of the Dalgleish name was George Dalgleish, the servant who, along with his master James Hepburn, 4th Earl of Bothwell, was instrumental in the mysterious murder of Henry Stuart, Lord Darnley, husband of the ill-fated Mary, Queen of Scots.

Although the exact circumstances surrounding the assassination are still shrouded in mystery more than 450 years after the event, what is known is that Bothwell was the arch-conspirator, assisted by a number of lesser-known figures, such as his servant George Dalgleish.

It was on the evening of February 9, 1567, that a tremendous explosion rudely awoke Edinburgh.

Kirk o' Field, a house just within the city walls, had been blown to smithereens, while the bodies of Darnley and his servant were later found in the garden.

Darnley, suffering from what in all probability was syphilis, had been lodged in Kirk o' Field while Mary and her infant son, the future James VI, were in residence at the Palace of Holyrood.

The queen had attended a wedding breakfast at Holyrood for one of her ladies-in-waiting, visiting her husband briefly before returning to the palace for the wedding masque.

In the intervening period the cellar of Kirk o' Field had been packed with gunpowder, furtively transported there by Dalgleish and others.

When the corpses of Darnley and his servant were discovered, it was noticed both were unmarked by the tremendous blast, and that they had been either strangled or smothered as they attempted to make their escape after belatedly realising their lives were in danger.

Bothwell, who later took the twice-widowed Mary's hand in marriage, was controversially acquitted of having had any part in 'the cruel, odious, treasonable and abominable slaughter' of Darnley, but less powerful figures implicated in the murder, such as George Dalgleish, were subsequently brought to justice and executed.

Along with fellow servants of Bothwell including John Hepburn, John Hay and William Powrie, he was hanged, drawn and quartered and his head set on Edinburgh's Netherbow Gate.

A series of incriminating letters between Bothwell and Mary, known as the Casket Letters, suggest the queen may have been implicated in the

Mary, Queen of Scots

plot to murder her husband, but controversy still rages as to the authenticity of the letters – while it is Dalgleish who is thought to have passed them to the Earl of Morton on his master's instruction.

Mary was later compelled to abdicate in favour of her son by a body known as the Confederate Lords and, following imprisonment for a time in Lochleven Castle and defeat at the battle of Langside, near Glasgow, on May 23, 1568, forced to flee into what she then naively thought would be the protection of England's Queen Elizabeth.

But she was instead fated for confinement in a succession of strongholds before her execution on February 8, 1587, in the Great Hall of Fotheringhay Castle, in Northamptonshire.

Bothwell, meanwhile, had fled to Scandinavia before the battle of Langside; reaching what he thought would be the sanctuary of Denmark, he was instead imprisoned in appalling conditions in Copenhagen's Dragsholm Castle, where he died in 1578.

In later centuries and rather more peaceful times and with the popular spelling variant 'Dalglish', Robert Dalglish was the colourful Scottish Radical politician born in Glasgow in 1808.

The son of a muslin manufacturer, calico printer and former Lord Provost of Glasgow, also named Robert Dalglish, despite his wealth and social status he campaigned for a much wider extension of the right to vote.

Independent Radical MP (Member of Parliament) for the city from 1857 to 1874, he was popular not only with those who voted for him, but also fellow MPs.

One contemporary commentator noted of him in 1873, seven years before his death:

"Popularity is commonly but a poor test of merit, yet in Parliament it has a distinct value and meaning, so that Mr Dalglish may well be proud of being known as the most popular Member of the House of Commons."

Obviously very much a sociable character, the commentator further wrote of him:

"He possesses the charity that is not puffed up, he is an easy-going, good-natured man, he is fond of the fair sex, he gives good dinners, and yet at the same time he has a sound judgement and discretion, often appealed to by men whose names are more frequently before the public."

High praise indeed.

Chapter four:

On the world stage

While bearers of the Dalgleish name experienced warfare on the actual battlefield, others have been at the forefront of bringing it to participants from the comfort of their homes in the form of computer gaming.

Born in Aberdeen in 1945, **Tom Dalgleish** is the pioneering designer of war gaming and other fantasy role playing materials such as *War of 1812*, *Napoleon*, *Hammer of the Scots*, *Klondyke* and *Eagles*.

His career in the complex world of gaming had a rather unusual genesis – through playing poker, he says, while serving as a midshipman in the British Merchant Navy.

Immigrating to Canada when aged 22, he teamed up five years later with Lance Gutteridge and Steve Brewster to form the gaming company Gamma Two Games which, in 1982, became Columbia Games – now run by Dalgleish and his son Grant from headquarters in Blaine, Washington.

A business partner for a time with N. Robin

Crossby, they developed the Hârn series that includes, from 1986, the sourcebook *Kanday*, the 1987 *Melderyn* and, from 1988, *Pilots' Almanac*.

Along with his son, he designed *Wizard Kings* and, with Jerry Taylor, *Hammer of the Scots* – with the latter board game the winner in 2004 of Games 100's Top 100 Games of the Year in the category of best historical simulation.

Still in the world of gaming, **Ben Daglish** was the musician and composer of soundtracks for games including *The Last Ninja*, *Deflektor* and *Trap*.

Born in London in 1966 but raised in Sheffield, he formed along with fellow musician and programmer Tony Crowther W.E.M.U.S.I.C. (We Make Use of Sound in Computers), while he also performed before his death in 2018 at computer games' events in the band SID80s.

From pioneers of computer gaming to pioneers in the field of medicine, **Professor Andrew Dalgleish** is the oncologist responsible for advances in the treatment of HIV/AIDS.

Born in 1950 and the holder of qualifications including Bachelor of Medicine and a Bachelor of Surgery degree from University College London, he served for a time in Australia with the Royal Flying Doctor Service before studying at the Institute for Cancer Research in Sydney.

Returning to the UK in 1984 at the Institute for Cancer Research, London, he was instrumental in helping to identify CD4 as the major cellular receptor for HIV.

Holding a number of positions including Foundation Professor of Oncology at St George's University of London, he is also a Fellow of, among others, the Academy of Medical Sciences and the Royal College of Physicians.

In the political field, as a Eurosceptic he campaigned for Britain to leave the European Union as a member of UKIP (United Kingdom Independence Party).

Yet another pioneer, this time in the field of children's historical fiction, **Alice Dalgliesh** was born in 1893 in Trinidad, British West Indies.

Immigrating to Britain with her family when aged 16, and to the United States six years later and eventually taking American citizenship, she studied kindergarten education at the Pratt Institute, New York.

Graduating from the Teachers College at

Columbia University as a Bachelor in Education and with a Master in English Literature, after teaching for a time she was invited in 1934 to launch a children's book publishing arm of Charles Scribner and Sons.

As its children's books editor until 1960, she developed juvenile science fiction – most notably as editor of Robert A. Heinlein's early work including his 1949 *Red Planet* and, from 1959, *Have Space Suit – Will Travel*.

A best-selling author in her own right, three of her books – *The Silver Pencil*, *The Bears of Hemlock Mountain* and *The Courage of Sarah Noble* – were runners-up for the American Library Association's prestigious Newbery Medal, now the Newbery Honor Medal.

Also with a number of her books named as Best Book of the Year by *Horn* magazine and many inspired by her love of American history, she died in 1979.

Not only an author but a noted engraver and books illustrator, **Eric Daglish** was born in 1892 in Islington, London but spent much of his working life in Buckinghamshire.

A lecturer for a time in zoology at Toynbee Hall, London and a member of the Society of Wood

Engravers – having been taught the art by his friend Paul Nash – he illustrated classic works including Izaak Walton's *Compleat Angler* and ones by the naturalist W.H. Hudson.

As both author and engraver, he illustrated his 1948 book *The Birds of the British Isles* with 48 engravings, while the cover featured coloured wood engravings of goldfinches.

He died in 1966, with many of his engravings now in the care of institutions including the British Museum and the Metropolitan Museum of New York, while his son **Stephen Daglish** has published work concerning his endeavours in tracing the origins of the Daglish family name.

In the field of Biblical studies and on American shores, **Edward Dalglish** was the prominent scholar born in 1909.

Educated in theology at a number of institutions including Union Theological Seminary, New York and Episcopal Theological Seminary, University of London, he served from 1952 until 1966 as professor of Old Testament and Hebrew at Eastern Baptist Theological Seminary, Pennsylvania.

It was while at the latter institution that he was a member of the team that undertook the translation work for the *New American Bible*; the author of 400 articles in *The Interpreter's Dictionary of the Bible* (*IDB*), he died in 2000.

Bearers of the Dalgleish name and its popular spelling variants have also excelled in the highly competitive world of sport.

Known as 'King Kenny', or 'King of the Kop' by generations of Liverpool supporters, **Kenny Dalglish** – more properly known as Sir Kenneth Mathieson Dalglish – is the Scottish former footballer and manager born in 1951 in the Dalmarnock area of Glasgow.

The son of an engineer and later moving with his family to the Govan area of the city, close to Ibrox Stadium, home of Rangers Football Club, this is the team he grew up supporting.

This was rather ironical – in view of the fact he would later become not only a Liverpool legend but also of Rangers' Old Firm rival Celtic.

After showing talent as a schoolboy player, he accrued a mass of championship wins and honours as both a player and manager.

In addition to earning more than 100 caps for his national team – scoring 30 goals between 1971 and 1986 – he won four Scottish Cups, one Scottish

League Cup and four Scottish League Championships with Celtic between 1971 and 1977.

With Liverpool – whose stadium is fondly known as 'The Kop' – he won an astonishing six English League Championships, four League Cups, the FA Cup, five Charity Shields, three European Cups and one European Super Cup.

Player-manager for a time with Liverpool and director of football at Celtic from 1999 to 2000, he is the recipient of honours and awards that include induction into both the Scottish and English Football Halls of Fame, ranked in 2006 at No.1 in a Liverpool fans' poll of "100 Players who Shook the Kop" and hailed by some as "the greatest striker in post-war British football."

Married to his wife Marina since 1974, the couple set up the Marina Dalglish Appeal in 2004 to raise money to treat cancer, following her successful treatment for the disease.

Also the recipient of an MBE for services to football and appointed a Knight Bachelor in 2018 for services to football, charity and the City of Liverpool, while in hospital in 2020, being treated for an unrelated condition, he tested positive for COVID-19, but it transpired he was asymptomatic.